CATHOLICISM
THE PIVOTAL PLAYERS

St. Augustine & St. Benedict

Dear Friends,

To be holy is to be like Christ. The call to holiness is universal, which means that holiness is not meant for only a privileged few, but it is the mission towards which all Christ's disciples should aspire. Those who aspire to holiness will become for others a way of knowing Christ, for Christ introduces himself to the world, not merely in abstractions or emotions or institutions, but through the people he has called to be his friends. As such, the presence of Christ is embodied in the lives of real people, in men and women who know Christ and through lives made distinct by their relationship with Christ, seek to introduce him to the world.

The saints are exemplars of holiness par excellence. In their lives the form of Christ takes shape and becomes tangible to the world. The world will experience in the saint a person, who like Christ, is both ordinary and extraordinary. To encounter a saint is to experience the natural as imbued with the supernatural, virtues are elevated by divine grace, and human weakness is overcome by an uncanny strength. The saint becomes for the Church and the world an exemplification of what holiness really and truly means, and from their witness all disciples discern their own call to holiness.

Not all who know Christ will manifest the heroic virtue that makes one a saint, but all Christians are gifted with the potential for mighty deeds and can contribute, in accord with their state of life, to the transformation of all things in Christ. For some, this work of transformation will reveal itself to the world in readily apparent ways, and for others it will remain hidden, but whether apparent or hidden, it is Christ who is present, active, and working.

CATHOLICISM: The Pivotal Players has been created as a tribute to those men and women whose friendship with Christ transformed not only their own lives, but also the world. The first of the Pivotal Players in Volume II are St. Augustine and St. Benedict, who both contributed to the continuation and preservation of Western Civilization after the fall of Rome.

CATHOLICISM: The Pivotal Players displays the potential that friendship with Christ unleashes in the lives of his disciples. It is my hope that those who view *CATHOLICISM: The Pivotal Players* will discover in these men and women not just people to be admired, but an invitation to accept as their own the universal call to holiness.

Peace,

+ Robert Barron

Bishop Robert Barron
Founder, Word on Fire
Auxiliary Bishop of Los Angeles

WORDonFIRE

www.WordOnFire.org • www.PivotalPlayers.com

CATHOLICISM

THE PIVOTAL PLAYERS

St. Augustine & St. Benedict

Study Guide

BASED ON THE SERIES CREATED BY

Bishop Robert Barron

AUTHORS

Chad C. Pecknold & Abbott Jeremy Driscoll

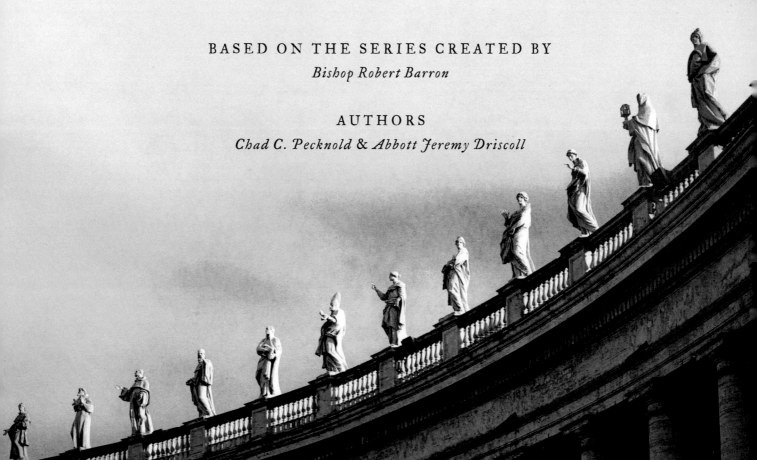

TABLE *of* CONTENTS

ST. AUGUSTINE

The Teacher

PART I - *Page* 1
PART II - *Page* 17
GLOSSARY - *Page* 35

ST. BENEDICT

The Monk

PART I - *Page* 37
PART II - *Page* 55
GLOSSARY - *Page* 73

CATHOLICISM
THE PIVOTAL PLAYERS
St. Augustine & St. Benedict

ST. AUGUSTINE

The Teacher

CATHOLICISM
THE PIVOTAL PLAYERS

St. Augustine Study Guide written by Chad C. Pecknold, Ph.D.

✚

ST. AUGUSTINE
The Teacher

STUDY GUIDE WRITTEN BY
Chad C. Pecknold, Ph.D.

Dr. Chad Pecknold serves on the faculty of The Catholic University of America in Washington D.C. as an Associate Professor of Systematic Theology. He joined the faculty in 2008 after earning his PhD from the University of Cambridge (UK). Dr. Pecknold teaches courses on fundamental theology, Christian anthropology, and political theology. He is the author of *Christianity and Politics: A Brief Guide to the History* (Cascade 2010), *The T&T Clark Companion to Augustine and Modern Theology* (Bloomsbury, 2014). He contributes frequently to debates in the public square, writing regularly for *The Wall Street Journal, First Things* and *National Review* on religion and politics. Pecknold has been quoted in hundreds of news outlets around the world and has appeared as a guest on radio and television shows such as NPR's "All Things Considered," BBC World News, and ABC News. He is a regular contributor to EWTN News Nightly. Professor Pecknold is currently writing a book on St. Augustine's *City of God.*

ST. AUGUSTINE

The Teacher

VIDEO OUTLINE—PART I

I.   INTRODUCTION

    A. Most significant bridge between culture of ancient Rome and Christian culture that would flower in Middle Ages

    B. Articulated Trinitarian theology

    C. Created discipline of philosophy of history and genre of autobiography

    D. Still greatly influences contemporary generations

II. THE *CONFESSIONS*

    A. Autobiographical work

        1. Introspective analogy of mind, intention, and aspiration

        2. Self portrait of a soul; a prayer overheard

        3. Combination of high intellectualism and profound emotion

        4. Key thesis: "Lord, you have made us for yourself; therefore, our heart is restless until it rests in you."

    B. Early Life

        1. Born 354 AD in Thagaste, North Africa in a Roman province

        2. Son of pagan man, Patricius, and Christian woman, Monica

        3. Instructed in Christianity, but not committed

        4. Longed to be master of spoken word

    C. Formative Years

        1. Stolen pear shows soul of fallen man

        2. Studied rhetoric in Carthage and immersed himself in sensual atmosphere

        3. Lived with a woman and fathered a son at 17 named Adeodatus

        4. Committed to leading the philosophical life

        5. Became a devotee of Manicheaism: battle between good and evil represented by spirit and matter

          a. Heretical sect

          b. Prompted Monica to pray in earnest for his conversion to Christianity

D. Life in Milan

    1. Appointed professor of rhetoric

    2. Greatly influenced by St. Ambrose

        a. Neo-platonic philosophy

        b. Allegorical, not literal, reading of Scripture

    3. Walked by a drunken man and thought, "Tomorrow that man will be sober but I will still be drunk on ambition."

    4. Studied Gospel of John and writings of St. Paul

    5. Heard child saying, "Take up and read." He took up the Bible and opened it randomly to read St. Paul's words "Put on the Lord Jesus Christ…"

    6. Spent a few months at an estate outside Milan, writing

    7. Baptized in Milan by St. Ambrose at Easter Vigil in 387

E. Return to Africa

    1. Left career in rhetoric and decided to return home

    2. Experienced shared vision of heaven with Monica a few days before her death

    3. Returned to Thagaste with his son and some disciples; established a Christian philosophical school

    4. While visiting Hippo, people pressed him into service as their priest

    5. Gained reputation as master preacher and skilled administrator

    6. Took over when Bishop of Hippo died and served as bishop from 395 until his death

F. Writings and Challenges while Bishop

    1. Wrote the *Confessions, The City of God,* and *De Trinitate* from 412-428

    2. Battled Donatists who believed that the moral quality of a minister of a sacrament determined its validity

    3. Struggles with Pelagians occupied last years of his life

    4. Spent last days meditating on psalms of repentance and died in 430

ST. AUGUSTINE

LIFE AND TIMES

There are many saints and martyrs in the early Church worthy of our admiration. Yet among the whole range of Latin Fathers there is one who reaches truly incomparable heights. Like Plato, Cicero, and the Apostle Paul all rolled into one, Augustine is truly a pivotal player in the story of human civilization, and in the story of the Church. At the heart of this pivotal player's story is the truth about God's grace running ahead of us in order to convert us to himself.

The Roman Empire had slowly moved from being a persecutor of Christianity to its ostensible promoter. While Emperor Constantine's Edict of Milan in 313 AD brought early Church persecution to an official end, pagan resentments towards Christianity remained. Augustine was thus born into a culture that still had one foot in the pagan world—filled with devotion to as many gods as there are daily tasks—and one foot in the new Christian world coming into being, which would become the official religion of the empire under Emperor Theodosius in 380 AD, shortly before Augustine's baptism. For these reasons, and more, that Augustine's life bears within it the mark of a world in the process of being converted to Christ.

Born in 354 AD to a pious Catholic woman named Monica and a pagan man named Patricius, Augustine was born between these two worlds. While not wealthy, Patricius was influential in the government of the city of Thagaste in North Africa and had great ambitions for his gifted son. Monica wanted nothing more for her husband and son than the Christian faith. Her husband eventually converted on his deathbed when Augustine was still a teenager. It would take nearly two decades of prayer before Monica would see her son confess the one, true Faith.

After the death of Patricius, a wealthy family friend arranged for the young Augustine to go to Carthage for an elite education in Rhetoric—a ticket to imperial influence, pagan vice, and a nine-year journey into a gnostic sect called Manichaeism. This heresy proclaimed that created matter was a shackle from which the soul must be freed. Augustine took a common law wife and at the young age of 17, he fathered a son with her, whom they named Adeodatus.

He distinguished himself in rhetoric at Carthage, and then returned to Thagaste preaching Manichaeism, even to his own Catholic mother. At 18 he read Cicero's *Hortensius*, which set him on a path towards wisdom, as he tells us in the third book of the *Confessions*. He returned to Carthage and over the course of a decade his doubts and disillusionment with Manicheanism increased.

A skeptical Augustine travelled to Rome, where he gained the attention of the Prefect, Symmachus, who appointed him "Public Orator" in Milan. While imperial rhetor in Milan from 384 to 387, he immersed himself in Neo-Platonic philosophy and for the first time became intellectually interested in Christianity. Ironically, it was at the pinnacle of Augustine's imperial career as a rhetorician that he came to look upon rhetoric as "a chair of lies," and was restless for the truth.

In late summer of 386 A.D., Augustine wept in a Milanese garden as he read the Apostle Paul's Letter to the Romans (see *Confessions* 8). As he became convinced of the truth of Christianity, his life took a profoundly new turn. He gathered a group of friends to study the Catholic faith at nearby Cassiciacum for six months. At the Easter Vigil on April 24, 387 A.D., God answered the life-long prayer of his mother when Ambrose, bishop of Milan, immersed Augustine in the cathedral's baptismal waters, baptizing him in the Name of the Father, and of the Son, and of the Holy Spirit.

Augustine was now a Catholic Christian. He traveled with his mother back to North Africa, and by 388, he had established a monastic community. He wrote a "Rule" for that community, which added to the foundation of Western monasticism. Within a few years, however, Augustine was pressed by fellow Catholics to preach and celebrate for them the sacred mysteries, and so he was ordained to the priesthood in 391. Then, by God's providence, he was elevated to bishop of Hippo in 395.

Over the next 35 years, Augustine wrote millions of words, fighting heresies from Manichaeism to Donatism to Pelagianism, always proclaiming the truth of the Catholic faith. His most celebrated works span the course of his episcopal career, first writing *Confessions*, and then his massive *City of God* and *On the Trinity*. He died in 430 AD at the age of 75. Never has a generation passed that has not been enthralled and challenged by what Augustine left behind.

CONFESSIONS

Augustine wrote *Confessions* not as "autobiography"—though this work will inspired the development of the genre—but as a penitential prayer, which lifts up every part of his life to God. It is a rhetorical masterpiece of high Latin style placed for the first time in the mode of an intimate, personal address to the One who made him. It is quite literally a confession of sin—original and actual—as well as a confession of the gift of faith that God gave to Augustine. Written two years into his apostolic ministry as a bishop in the Catholic Church, we should understand *Confessions* as an integral part of his episcopal witness throughout the Roman Empire.

While the *Confessions* focuses on the inner life of Augustine, what he tells us is instructive for thinking about our lives too. We should think of it as an *Itinerarium Mentis in Deum*—as the "mind's journey into God." What makes *Confessions* extraordinary is that Augustine captures something timeless and universal through the particular, interior movements of his own soul. As a result, the work remains fresh, and refreshing. In every age, it speaks to every man as though it were his very own story. It's not just Augustine's story. It's the story of the conversion of the whole Western world. It's about our conversion. It's the archetype of the very drama of the human soul laid bare before God.

For this reason, *Confessions* is rightly summarized through its most famous line, found on the very first page of the book: *Fecisti nos ad te, Domine, et inquietum est cor nostrum donec requiescat in te.* "You have made us for yourself, Lord, and our hearts are restless until they rest in You."

What is often missed, however, is that Augustine precedes these lines with a recognition that it is God who moves us towards Him. "You stir us to take pleasure in praising You." While we are born with a natural desire for God—a capacity that makes us restless for an end far greater than we can imagine—we chase a thousand different ends searching for him. All our highest aims in this life run on this restless power. But it is only by God "stirring us," acting upon the receptive soul, that we are brought into a communion that gives the soul the pleasure of praising God. The right praise of God is the most proper and highest end for which we were made, and that unites us to the happiness that cannot be lost.

These crucial opening lines work like a thesis in the great song of the *Confessions*: our longing for God, our eternal "homesickness," our nagging sense of being lost or estranged from God, as well as our need to be found and born from above. The reader finds herself implicated from the outset in a kind of universal examination of conscience and memory. Though Augustine asks questions of himself, the reader can hardly help but to participate in a similar search for truth.

The structure of the work is elegant, with nine books recounting the various intellectual, moral, and spiritual conversions of his own life, and four books turning our attention to the more universal question of the conversion of creation, memory, and time itself. While some readers puzzle over how the books cohere, it's quite clear that Augustine is leading the reader progressively through the particularities of his own life as a microcosm of creation itself—"a little piece of creation" through which we might come to understand the whole. He remembers what is past and describes what is present in order to refer us to a future hope of eternal life.

In Book One, he introduces us to his childhood and begins the itinerary of his soul's journey. He is a keen observer of the infant, who displays even at his mother's breast a kind of envy for the sibling.

This is not voluntary in the infant, so it must be something more primal. It is, of course, evidence of an "original sin" which can be seen even among the "innocent." His own disobedience towards his parents and teachers opens up the question of why human beings have a tendency towards disobedience of any sort. What causes that? Does it have a cause?

Similarly, we can observe in a child learning a language a certain inadequacy. We have a capacity for language, and we enter into relationships through words.

But we begin with a certain privation, a lack and a need, for something greater than ourselves, which must be sought through learning over time. He will develop this theme in another work written at roughly the same time. In *De Doctrina Christiana* ("On Christian Teaching"), Augustine elaborates on the importance of understanding language as signs that refer us to things, and the sacraments of the Church as visible signs that unite us to invisible realities on our pilgrimage toward heaven, the fulfillment of the City of God.

Confessions shows us the nature of that pilgrimage. We see the searching restlessness of reason just as we see the way a saint confesses sin. He is given the finest education, and yet experiences an emptiness in knowledge. He learns how to use rhetoric to move the passions of his listeners, but laments that he moves them toward either what is fleeting, insubstantial, or immoral. He grieves his own sins as a sign of a fundamental lack of the goodness he desires, and even grieves the impermanence and misdirection that occurred in his pursuit of the good.

In Book Two, we find one of the most famous scenes of his life from the period of his adolescence. Augustine famously recounts how he trespasses to steal a pear that is not his, that is not ripe, and that he neither wants nor needs. It is rightly famous because it confesses the fundamental absurdity of sin as a flight from reason. Augustine wonders why his teenage self stole the pear and can find no good reason. That is because sin is never anything more than a "*privatio boni*," a privation of the good without cause or reason. Thus, the stolen pear story gives us a powerful image of disobedience and transgression, which, in Augustine's view, are always irrational and contrary to creation.

Book Three leads us along the same penitential path, one already hinted at in his lament about the emptiness of his learning in Book One. This path leads him through a series of intellectual conversions that begin with his discovery of philosophy through Cicero's now lost *Hortensius*—a work he read as a teenager, and that he credits with exciting him to the love of a wisdom greater than mere knowledge.

One finds Augustine confessing something like intellectual pride as he traverses his way, over a decade, into and out of Manichaeism, which imagined the material world itself as a fall from immaterial light. To be free from the shackles of our embodied created nature, Manichaeans promised liberation through secret knowledge (*gnosis*) of immaterial truths. They advocated abstaining from eating meat and having procreative sex, denying the very goodness of nature and reproduction themselves. They believed in something like the "total depravity" of matter.

Perhaps his disillusionment with Manichaeism drove him into academic skepticism for a time. By Book Seven, we can see that it's the teachings of Plato—rediscovered through a philosophical circle of Roman Neoplatonists in Milan—that help him recover from gnostic ideology and bring him to the cusp of Christianity. We begin to see how he aligns certain Neoplatonic teachings about intellectual illumination with St. John the Evangelist's teaching about Jesus as the Light illumining the world. The Platonists seemed to understand that happiness could only be found in intellectual, contemplative union with the very *Logos* or mind of God. Yet Augustine begins to see clearly that, as close as they may be to the truth, the *Platonici* utterly fail to grasp that Jesus was the *Logos* made flesh. The Platonists could see well enough that God was the end of man's desire to know, but they could not see that Jesus Christ was himself that end, and the means by which we may be joined to our highest end in God.

SAINT MONICA

Monica was born in 333 in Thagaste, Africa, which is now Algeria. Her Christian parents raised her in the faith but arranged for her to marry a pagan official, Patricius, at a young age. Monica lived with Patricius and his mother and bore three children who lived past infancy: Augustine, Navigius, and Perpetua.

Both Patricius and his mother were ill-tempered and prone to violence, vocally disapproving of Monica's life of prayer and charity. However, for some reason, Patricius always had a great respect for her, and when Augustine fell ill, Patricius gave consent for Augustine to be baptized; however, when Augustine recovered, Patricius rescinded his consent. Monica's prayers, good deeds, and steadfast example of Christian faith finally won over her husband and his mother, and they were both baptized a year before Patricius' death.

Augustine was 17 when his father died and was sent to Carthage to study rhetoric. Navigius and Perpetua entered religious life, while Augustine took the secular path of self-love. His dissolute lifestyle tore at Monica's heart, and she started to pray fervently for his conversion.

Her prayer would go on for years until he was finally baptized in Milan at the age of 32.

Monica worked diligently to stay close to Augustine, following him to Rome and then to Milan, often against his will. St. Ambrose, the bishop of Milan, was her spiritual advisor and most likely joined in her prayers for Augustine's conversion. She accompanied her son and grandson to Cassiciacum, outside of Milan, for six months before Augustine's baptism. Soon after the baptism, they decided to return to Africa, but she became ill in the ancient port of Ostia before setting sail for Africa and, after nine days with a fever, she died.

In the *Confessions*, Augustine recorded her words right before her death: "Son, nothing in this world now affords me delight. I do not know what there is now left for me to do or why I am still here, all my hopes in this world being now fulfilled."

She was buried at Ostia and was virtually forgotten until 1430, when Pope Martin V had her relics moved to Rome. Reports of many miracles surfaced while the relics made their way to Rome, and the cult of St. Monica began to emerge. Later, Cardinal d'Estouteville, archbishop of Rouen, France, built a church to honor St. Augustine, and Monica's relics were moved to a chapel there.

St. Monica is also venerated among Orthodox Christians and is the patron saint of mothers, married women, and abuse victims. Her feast day is August 27.

It's in Book Eight that we find Augustine under a fig tree in a Milanese garden, hearing children singing *"Tolle lege, tolle lege,"* or "take up and read, take up and read." Hearing the words of this nursery-school sing-song as a sign from God, he picked up the Apostle Paul's Letter to the Romans. His eyes flooded with tears as he read that other famous convert, Saint Paul, admonishing him "to put on the Lord Jesus Christ and make no provision for the flesh, to gratify its desires" (Romans 13:14). What the Manichaeans denied, and what the Platonists could only partly affirm, was the longing for the redemption of material creation itself. Original sin had not harmed the goodness of our created nature as such, as the Manichaeans believed, but it had had destroyed our original harmony with God, and so weakened our inclination to virtue and holiness. Augustine saw clearly that this wound could only be healed through incorporation into Christ's sinless body. Union with Christ alone can free us from original sin and the disordered desires of the flesh due to a weakened will.

In the ninth book, we find Augustine speaking of his baptism in passing, as a sacrament sealing the reality of his own interior conversion in Milan. Instead of attending to his baptism in any detail, Augustine gives the reader insight into the greater mysteries that he is able to see now through his spiritual rebirth. What may surprise readers is that much of what he sees comes to us through a recounting of the life of his mother. Most famously, it is his "vision at Ostia," which he experiences with his mother Monica. Together, on Roman shores, they are given a mystical vision of eternal joy, a happiness that can never be lost. It gives them both a profound confidence that their true home is not here, but in heaven, in the City of God. Progressively it seems that Augustine, concluding the story of his conversions, treats Monica as more than simply his earthly mother, but also as a spiritual mother—indeed as one whose intercessory prayers helped bring him to rebirth. While it is Monica whom he praises as an exemplar of Christian humility and obedience, and as one whose tireless intercessions had claimed him for the Church, his elevated descriptions of her at times makes her seem like a figure of the Blessed Mother, who does the same for all poor banished children of Eve.

There is much debate about what connects Books 1-9 and Books 10-13 of the *Confessions*. But the most obvious answer is also the most dependable: Book 10. If we lost track of the circuitous ascent of a soul into God in Books 1-9, Augustine makes it clear in Book 10 that it was only by being united to Jesus Christ that this "little piece of creation" can ascend at all. We do not rise by our own power, but by God's grace. He confesses "Late have I loved thee, O Beauty, ever ancient, ever new," precisely because he knows that he had come to love God because God had stirred him to take pleasure in praising Him.

After this partial vision of a single life converted by grace, Augustine wants the reader to begin afresh with an exegesis of Genesis, in order to think about memory and the purpose of the time we've been given. In the last three books, which are both biblical and philosophical, we glimpse the universal nature of our hunger for God as contingent creatures in need of a grace we cannot supply for ourselves, a redemption of our bodies beyond death, and a hope for the vision of God, which will give us eternal happiness.

CONVERSION PRAYER *of* ST. AUGUSTINE *from the* CONFESSIONS

Late have I loved Thee, O Beauty so ancient and so new;
late have I loved Thee!
For behold Thou wert within me, and I outside; and I
sought Thee outside and in my unloveliness fell upon
those lovely things that Thou hast made.
Thou wert with me and I was not with Thee.
I was kept from Thee by those things, yet had they not been in Thee,
they would not have been at all.
Thou didst call and cry to me and break open my deafness:
and Thou didst send forth Thy beams and shine upon me
and chase away my blindness:
Thou didst breathe fragrance upon me,
and I drew in my breath and do now pant for Thee:
I tasted Thee, and now hunger and thirst for Thee:
Thou didst touch me, and I have burned for Thy peace.

—from *Confessions*, Book 10, Chapter XXVII, pg. 258,
    Word on Fire Classics

QUESTIONS FOR UNDERSTANDING

1. What did looking back on his theft of a pear as an adolescent teach Augustine, according to his recounting of the story in *Confessions*? (Gen 3:1-5; CCC 1849-1850, 1871-1872)

2. Describe the two significant conversions Augustine embraced before his baptism. How did he eventually get to Christianity? (CCC 1954, 1956; 1 Tim 6:20-21)

3. What does Augustine believe is "the highest end for which we were made"? How did this "end" become evident to him? (Ex 20:1-6; CCC 2114)

4. How did Augustine's mother influence his life? What spiritual experience did they share toward the end of her life? What did that experience reveal to them? (Eph 6:18; CCC 2634-2635)

5. What does Augustine believe is the only way one soul, as a "little piece of creation," can "ascend" or be transformed to a higher level? (John 14:6; Rom 10:9-10; 2 Pet 1:3-4; CCC 460)

QUESTIONS FOR APPLICATION

1. Reflect on St. Augustine's famous adage: "Lord, you have made us for yourself; therefore, our heart is restless until it rests in you." Where in your life are you "restless"? What does "resting" in God mean to you?

2. What does the life of St. Monica teach you about living the Christian faith?

3. Reflect on the Conversion Prayer of St. Augustine (see sidebar page 12). What words or phrases stand out as most relevant in your own life? Why?

ST. AUGUSTINE

The Teacher

VIDEO OUTLINE—PART II

I. *THE CITY OF GOD*

   A. Overview

      1. Written to argue against the opinion that the fall of Rome was due to Rome's adoption of Christianity

      2. Augustine argued that Rome fell due to their worship of false gods and is an example of the Earthly City

         a. Based on immorality and violence of the Roman gods

         b. "Lust to dominate," not tranquility of order

         c. Grounded in self-love

         d. Illustrated by the founding myth of Romulus and Remus

      3. City of God is an alternative form of society

         a. Earthly community that mirrors the heavenly community, gathered in worship of the one, true God

         b. Often appears in the world as small and powerless

   B. City of God and Earthly City (City of Man) are intertwined in this world

      1. Found in the hearts of Christians and in the Church

      2. Continual conflict, but City of God always prevails in the end

      3. Augustine sees Christians as "resident aliens" in the world; pilgrims who are citizens of the City of God making their way through the Earthly City

   C. Just War Theory

      1. Augustine has strong prejudice against war and violence

      2. His moral acceptance of warfare under certain conditions is a concession to the sinful world and one way that citizens of the City of God make their way through the Earthly City

      3. Just war: must be fought for a morally, praiseworthy cause; declared by a competent authority; and combatants are fighting with the right intentions

D. Attributes of citizens of the City of God

II.   AGAINST THE PELAGIAN HERESY
    A. Pelagian Teaching
        1. Moral perfection can be achieved through our exercise of the will
        2. Denied original sin
        3. Humans can determine the meaning of their own life
        4. Undermines Christianity: leads to the idea that we do not need a Savior, just a moral teacher or guide

    B. Contemporary translation of Pelagian heresy
        1. Similar to addiction
        2. Condition in which we find ourselves that has rendered us helpless where something more powerful than free will is needed to overcome it
        3. Both sinner and addict have to turn their will over to a higher power; cannot solve the problem through our own efforts

III.   CONCLUSION
    A. Augustine has allowed people over the centuries to see their own stories of sin and grace in his story

    B. Showed us that we are citizens of a higher society based on the right praise of God

    C. Reminded us of the intractability of sin, which teaches us to look, not just for another teacher, but for a Savior

ST. AUGUSTINE

THE *CITY OF GOD* & AUGUSTINE AGAINST THE PELAGIANS

By the time the Visigoths sacked Rome in 410 A.D., Augustine's fame as a bishop had spread throughout the Roman empire. As news of the sack of Rome raced throughout the world, elite Romans still devoted to the gods of the old pagan religion took the opportunity to blame Rome's fall on Christianity. It fell to Augustine to defend the Catholic faith against the pagans.

At the same time, Augustine was battling a heresy within the Catholic Church called Pelagianism, which was a particularly "Roman" kind of heresy that denied original sin and claimed that human beings were capable of willing and doing the good on their own power, without God's help. It was a heresy that fit perfectly with Roman pride, honor, and self-sufficiency. But it was also a heresy that denied confession of sin, humility, conversion, and dependence on the grace of God in Jesus Christ. These same themes that mark his battles against error within the Church also mark his battles against error from without—as is evident in his massive work, *The City of God*.

Augustine's *De Civitate Dei Contra Paganos* spans 22 books, 1500 pages, and was written in stages over more than a decade—overlapping his battle against Pelagianism and his speculative work on God, *De Trinitate*. *The City of God*, is by Augustine's own admission, "a great and arduous work."

Augustine tells us in the preface that his friend Marcellinus had requested that the bishop offer a defense against the charge that Christianity was to blame for Rome's weakened position prior to the invasion of the Visigoths. Volusianus—a *pagan* imperial proconsul for Africa—had personally pressed these criticisms to Marcellinus—a *Christian* imperial

---

ST. AUGUSTINE: *The Teacher*

proconsul for Africa. Marcellinus wanted to know how to answer Volusianus. Once again, Augustine was between two worlds, but by now he confidently knew the world in which he stood.

The pagan criticism was that Rome's decline coincided with its conversion to Catholic Christianity. Augustine rebuked this criticism, as historical facts simply didn't match the accusation. For example, during the sack of Rome, citizens were only saved from Gothic captors by taking refuge in the sacred basilicas and churches of the saints and martyrs. "What ingratitude!", Augustine exclaimed, that Romans would take shelter under Christ but attack Christianity. From the outset, and with unrelenting depth of historical and logical argument, he demolishes the pagan charge.

Augustine answers the challenge even in the first book of the *City of God*: Rome did not fall because of the Visigoths, and even less because of Christianity. Rome fell, like any human thing, because of a fundamental disorder that marked it from the beginning.

One of the leitmotifs to illustrate this inherent disorder is the story of Remus and Romulus, the brothers who founded Rome. Though Romans weren't accustomed to seeing their origins this way, Augustine reminded his readers that Rome was founded on a terrible, murderous, fratricidal act. In the lust for total political domination, Romulus murdered his brother Remus at the founding of the city, which would subsequently take its name not from the slain brother but from the slayer. At several points (e.g., *City* 1.34; 3.6; 15.5) Augustine takes the opportunity to show the Romans the similarities between Remus and Romulus and the biblical brothers Cain and Abel, precisely to teach them about original sin—a loss of that original justice for which humanity was made. Augustine wants to make it clear that Rome's decline is not rooted in any historical turn to Christianity, but it is rooted in sin, violence, immorality, bad religion, and the weakness of the will that succumbs to the greedy and murderous lust to dominate others. Rome's decline, he argues, has come not from without but from within.

Against the common claim that Romans were stoical in the face of suffering, Augustine wants to reveal the weakness of Rome running deeply through a history of self-sufficient pride, which he contrasts with the strength of Christian humility. Christians face suffering by humble trust in divine providence—a theme concurrent with his anti-Pelagian writings.

Beyond Remus and Romulus and the early founding, Augustine also points to Roman heroes and heroines, some genuinely heroic (such as Regulus) and others who only seem so. He points to Lucretia as a so-called heroine of the late monarchical period who killed herself after being raped by one of Rome's princes. This injustice became a rallying point for Romans to overthrow the monarchy and establish a republic in 509 B.C. Lucretia killed herself to convince her fellow Romans she was innocent, to defend her honor. Augustine asks what kind of virtue responds to the injustice of rape with the even greater injustice of murder (*City* 1.29)? Where Romans saw Lucretia as a paragon of civic virtue in the face of suffering, Augustine wanted them to see in Lucretia a fallen emblem of a people who are self-destructive, suicidal, and truly without hope in the face of suffering. Romans have fallen not because of Christianity, but because of self-deluding pride.

Augustine wants to highlight the errant ways in which human beings are restless for God, precisely in order to prepare the reader to confess their own genuinely dire need of the truth, which can illumine darkness and restore health by God's grace.

As highlighted above, Augustine dismantles Rome's "fancy picture of itself" in the first five books, revealing how its "gods" never did Rome any temporal favors, and how, in fact, their own debauchery tended to degrade the moral imagination of the Roman people, evident through many vulgar theatrical plays about the gods. In the second five books, he shows how Rome's own best philosophers and natural theologians saw the gods as myths, tending to be intellectual "monotheists" who identified one God as the "soul of the world," condescending to tolerate the people's "gods" as "noble lies."

Augustine praises the Platonists—and more specifically Roman Neoplatonists—for seeing that the true God must transcend this world entirely as the supreme uncaused cause and end of all that exists. Book Eight provides a history of Greco-Roman philosophy that overwhelmingly favors this Platonic tendency towards monotheism. Yet Augustine is not uncritical of Platonists whom he praises for their intellectual achievement of arriving at certain knowledge of the true God. He criticizes all those philosophers who have knowledge of the one true God yet tolerate false ones. Augustine reasons that this tolerance of religious error is due to the fact that the truths they know about God are simply too weak to crush the theological errors of bad religion. Even at its greatest philosophical heights, Rome had failed to crush her own errors and vices, according to Augustine. This also fits with the anti-Pelagian theme that we cannot, even at the height of our intellectual powers, save ourselves. Roman religion has not strengthened or elevated Rome, either in temporal or eternal advantage. It certainly has not made Rome happy. Redemption must come from without.

In Book Ten, the Christological center of the City of God, the Roman reader is finally referred to Jesus Christ, the one true mediator who can unite Rome to her highest end. It is here, at the center of the great work, that Augustine aligns Christ's sacrifice with the sacrifice of the Most Holy Eucharist, and also with the sacrifices of saints and martyrs—the "*totus Christus*" or "total Christ," head and body, on earth as it is in heaven. It is here we have the image of a world rightly ordered through conformity to Christ who is the hope of humanity, and also the hope of Rome.

Where Remus and Romulus were marked overwhelmingly by the political desire to dominate, even to the point of fratricide, saints and apostles like Peter and Paul are marked overwhelmingly by faith in Jesus Christ, even to the point of martyrdom because they were formed by hope in bodily resurrection to eternal life. This is good news for Rome! If Rome adheres to Jesus Christ, rather than Cain or Romulus, they can be free from their fratricidal fall. Rome's redemption depends not on a return to paganism, but on full conversion and conformity to Christ. Rome's true fraternity is not founded on fratricide but only upon Christ's peace, which reconciles us to God, and makes us free citizens of his City. This is the true hope of Rome, which the Church proclaims.

In the second half of *The City of God*, Augustine takes his reader on a tour through Israel's history, showing them the origins, itineraries, and destinies of two cities formed by two loves. In one city, the citizens love God above themselves, and in the other, they love themselves above God. Cain and Abel, Sarah and Hagar, Babel and Jerusalem, the wheat and the tares—these are the biblical archetypes for two loves, two citizens, two cosmic cities. One city is formed by pride, the other by humility. One city begins in an absurd turn away from our highest good, and the other city begins by saying 'Yes' to God. In this way, the second half gives us a much deeper way of understanding how the two cities can be distinguished at the root of every interior disposition, in our actions and in history.

In Book Eleven, Augustine tells us the two cities really begin in the angelic community. Lucifer, whose name means "Light derived from God," falls in love with his own light rather than the Source of it. Absurdly wanting the light to be all his own, Lucifer turns away from the cause of his own derived existence. In a dazzling display of biblical interpretation, Augustine suggests that this is the absurd origin of the City of Man, which reflects the absurd human turn away from God in the Garden of Eden. As we also saw in his *Confessions*, obedience and trust in God is rational, and rebellious disobedience is irrational—a flight from the Logos. Our way back to God, then, requires healing our intellect and will, our mind as well as our passions.

Augustine develops his biblical understanding of the human person especially in Books 12-14, where he shows that the two cities are located primarily in the will, since it is the will that directs a person to their end (see *City* 12.1). Neither good and bad angels nor good and bad people differ by nature; they only differ by their wills, their desires. In this way, Augustine shows his disagreement with Manichaean dualism as he sees the fundamental goodness of our nature but locates the City of Man as a turn of the will away from God. In this way, the two cities always begin in the interior movements of the soul. Many have observed in this a

Platonic theme that saw a profound unity between the Soul, the City, and the Cosmos, but here it comes to us through his reading of the Book of Genesis. "Although the will derives its existence, as a nature, from its creation by God, its falling away from its true being is due to its creation out of nothing" (see *City* 14.13). It is thus important that we take our desires and passions seriously and examine how our will directs us. Book 14 rejects the Stoic view of the passions as "disturbances" from which we must be freed (a theme he also briefly addresses in Book Nine). The passions are created, so they must be good. Thus, the Christian must see the passions as capable of being rightly or wrongly ordered. Our desires may be wrongly disordered and consequently may disorder our actions. But Christians have help. We are not left with the option of either refusing our passions as disturbances or embracing our passions however badly they are ordered. God the Father has revealed to us how to re-order all emotions, passions, affections, and desires through the Passion of God the Son.

Books 15-18 treat the contrast of the two cities through the biblical story. While Cain founded an earthly city, Abel founded no city, but received his citizenship from above. Noah's Ark prefigures Christ and his Church, with the door likened to the wound in Christ's side through which some of creation may be saved. Tracing a kind of allegorical genealogy, Augustine sees archetypes of the two cities everywhere in Scripture, though often in complex ways that cannot be described as simply dualist.

In Book Sixteen, for example, Noah's three sons complicate the lineage of the chosen people, Israel, who are the citizens of the City of God on pilgrimage toward fulfillment in heaven. Shem stands for Israel's Anointed (Christ); Japheth means "enlargement" and so stands for the inclusion of the Gentiles as citizens of the City of God; and Ham means "hot" and so stands for those heretics who sometimes travel with, but will finally be separated from, the City of God. The contrast between the two cities are thus often instructive within the Church. As he puts it at the end of Book 18, while kings can persecute the body from without, heretics persecute the heart from within—yet both persecutions can train City of God citizens in wisdom.

While medieval readers often focused on Book 14, dealing with the passions of the soul, modern readers are most attracted to Book 19, concerning the right ordering of the city. Here Augustine completes an argument against Rome using Cicero's definition of republic, which he only briefly began in Book 2. Cicero's definition of a commonweal was a multitude "united in association by a common sense of right," which depends on justice and "justice is that virtue which assigns to everyone his due," so all rights flow from "the fount of justice" (see *City* 19.21). Augustine uses this definition to the Church's advantage. He argues that if this is what is required for "complete justice in supreme government," then Rome fails to be a republic because in addition to the history of Roman injustices, pagan Rome fails to render what is due to God.

Having taken away the Ciceronian definition and reserved it for the Church, which is constituted by the perfect justice achieved by Christ's sacrifice, readers could get the misimpression that Augustine sees the Church as a replacement for political communities—as if he believed in theocracy (absorption of the state into the Church) or as if he viewed the Church as "the best regime." But this is not what he means. Instead, what he imagines is two definitions of a "republic"—the first, or perfect republic, is perfect by virtue of Christ's rendering the perfect offering to God (on earth as it is in heaven). He posits an alternative definition of "republic" that involves a matter of degrees like a scale, which may move closer or further away from the highest good. The way you can evaluate republics with this alternative definition is through an analysis of their communal dispositions, the architecture of their appetites, the direction of their loves, and the relation of their liberties to truth, being, and reality. Augustine's alternative, scalar definition shows that a republic is "an association of rational beings united by a common agreement on the objects of their love" (see *City* 19.24).

Whether at the level of the city, the soul, or the cosmos itself, Augustine wants neither a Manichaean denial of our nature, a Stoic denial of our passions, or a Pelagian denial of God's grace. Rather Augustine consistently draws the reader to think about how our nature, our desires, and our cities should be rightly ordered, and they can only be rightly ordered if we willingly unite them to Jesus Christ.

As with the story of his soul in the *Confessions*, Augustine ends the *City of God* with a vision. It is a vision of separating the two cities—Books 20-22 concern judgment, eternal death or eternal life. Augustine believes that God has given humans free will, and many will refuse to become friends of God and thus will reap the consequences of being separated from God's love. But those who cooperate with God and whose wills have been conformed to the divine will in Jesus Christ, will be made citizens of the City of God eternally. Instead of being constituted by some minimal concord of human will, the City of God is constituted by nothing less than the happiness of seeing God face-to-face and knowing the perfect concord God intends for His creation. Now we are on pilgrimage to this City, and we see through a glass darkly. But then we shall see God, the happiness that can never be lost. "There we shall be still and see; we shall see and we shall love; we shall love and we shall praise." (see *City* 22.30)

Augustine shows the Christian how to look with equanimity upon both the virtues and vices of the soul and of the culture of a city, and from an eternal perspective find the ways in which every nation might know the excellence of humility that is receptive to the gift of faith, so that every person might have the hope of an eternal life of happiness.

JUST WAR DOCTRINE

There are traditionally two parts to the "Just War" doctrine: the right to go to war and the right conduct during war (e.g., the Geneva Conventions). Some have added a third category regarding the right conduct after the war ends. Many philosophers and theologians, including St. Augustine and St. Thomas Aquinas, have written about "just war." Military organizations and contemporary scholars have expanded upon these ideas, and there is still much debate about when and if to call a war "just."

Murray Rothbard, economist, historian, and political theorist, succinctly summarized the term: "*A just war exists when a people tries to ward off the threat of coercive domination by another people, or to overthrow an already-existing domination. A war is unjust, on the other hand, when a people try to impose domination on another people or try to retain an already existing coercive rule over them.*" (1)

Jonathan Riley-Smith writes in *Rethinking the Crusades*, "*The consensus among Christians on the use of violence has changed radically since the crusades were fought. The just war theory prevailing for most of the last two centuries—that violence is an evil that can, in certain situations, be condoned as the lesser of evils—is relatively young.*" The contemporary theory has rejected the older idea that "*violence could be employed on behalf of Christ's intentions for mankind and could even be directly authorized by him.*" (2)

Elements from the just war theory of Augustine's time that have survived and been incorporated into the Church's teaching today include:

1. A JUST AND MORAL REASON: Innocent life must be in grave danger and intervention must be needed to protect that life. St. Thomas Aquinas wrote that the war must occur for a "*good and just purpose rather than for self-gain or as an exercise of power.*" (3)

2. PROPER AUTHORITY: Only established, public authorities (e.g., legitimate governments) may wage war. The political authority must exist within a system that defines and allows interpretations of justice. Dictatorships and rogue states are not considered viable political authorities. Proper authority that carefully considers a declaration of war is what distinguishes war from murder.

3. RIGHT INTENTION: The Church believes all people and all governments should value and work to avoid war. *"However, as long as the danger of war persists and there is no international authority with the necessary competence and power, governments cannot be denied the right of lawful self-defense, once all peace efforts have failed"* (CCC 2308).

4. PROPORTIONALITY: violence used in war must be proportional to specific, military objectives.

> *Every act of war directed to the indiscriminate destruction of whole cities or vast areas with their inhabitants is a crime against God and man, which merits firm and unequivocal condemnation. A danger of modern warfare is that it provides the opportunity to those who possess modern scientific weapons—especially atomic, biological, or chemical weapons—to commit such crimes.* (CCC 2314)

In summary, a "just war" in the Church's opinion is based on self-defense and decisions to enter into that war are subject to "rigorous conditions of moral legitimacy" (CCC 2309). The elements to consider in defining a war as just and necessary for self-defense include:

- *the damage inflicted by the aggressor on the nation or community of nations must be lasting, grave, and certain;*

- *all other means of putting an end to it must have been shown to be impractical or ineffective;*

- *there must be serious prospects of success;*

- *the use of arms must not produce evils and disorders graver than the evil to be eliminated.*

(CCC 2309)

QUESTIONS FOR UNDERSTANDING

1. How does the myth of Romulus and Remus provide insight about the values of ancient Rome? What Biblical story is the myth's counterpart? In comparing these two stories, what is the difference in the outcome and how does that difference help define the two cities Augustine describes? (Gen 4:1-17; CCC 2258-2260)

2. Describe St. Augustine's view that bad worship leads to bad government. (CCC 2110-2114, 2244, 2286)

3. What does it mean to be a "resident alien" or pilgrim on earth, according to Augustine? How are "resident aliens" supposed to react to civic authority? (Jer 27:6-8, 29:4-14; 1 Pet 2:11-17; CCC 2238-2240)

4. What are the characteristics of citizens of the City of God? (Matt 22:36-40; Matt 10:37-39; Gal 5:19-26; CCC 2256)

5. Are passions good or evil? Explain. (CCC 1767-1769)

6. What is the "just war doctrine"? What circumstances need to be present for killing someone in conflict and not violating the 5th commandment? (Rom 13:3-7; CCC 2302-2317)

QUESTIONS FOR APPLICATION

1. How is the tension between the City of God and the City of Man evident in our culture today?

2. Where in your own soul do you see conflicts between the two cities?

3. Describe times when the same passion or desire within you has led to good and when it has led to sinful behavior.

✠
BIBLIOGRAPHY

Cavadini, John. "Eucharistic Exegesis in Augustine's Confessions." *Augustinian Studies* 41, no. 1 (2010): 87-108.

Dodaro, Robert. *Christ and the Just Society in the Thought of Augustine.* Cambridge: Cambridge University Press, 2006.

Harrison, Carole. *Rethinking Augustine's Early Works: An Argument for Continuity.* Oxford: Oxford University Press, 2006.

Levering, Matthew. *The Theology of Augustine: An Introductory Guide to His Most Important Works.* Grand Rapids, MI: Baker Academic, 2016.

O'Daly, Gerard. *Augustine's City of God: A Reader's Guide.* Oxford: Oxford University Press, 2004.

Ortiz, Jared. *"You Made Us For Yourself": Creation in St. Augustine's Confessions.* Minneapolis, MN: Fortress Press, 2016.

"Just War" Sidebar Bibliography:

1. Murray N. Rothbard's presentation at the Mises Institute's Costs of War conference in Atlanta, May 1994.

2. *Smith, Jonathan R. "Rethinking the Crusades". Catholic Education Resource Center.*

3. Thomas Aquinas, *Summa Theologica* – Q. 40 Article 1

✝

GLOSSARY

ADEODATUS: The son of Augustine and his common-law wife, who is unnamed in the *Confessions*. Adeodatus lived and traveled with Augustine in Milan and later back to Africa.

CICERO: Marcus Tullius Cicero (106 BC – 43 BC) was a Roman statesman, orator, lawyer, and philosopher, who once held the highest elected political office in Rome. Cicero introduced the Romans to the chief schools of Greek philosophy and created a Latin philosophical vocabulary. Though he was an accomplished orator and successful lawyer, Cicero believed his political career was his most important achievement. St. Augustine credits Cicero's *Hortensius* for his lifelong dedication to philosophy, the pursuit of wisdom.

DONATISM: Heresy claiming that the moral character of the priest or minister determined the efficacy of the sacrament he administered. The Church denied this claim, professing that the efficacy of the sacrament was the grace of God, which did not vary depending on the morality of the minister.

HERESY: "The obstinate, post-baptismal denial of some truth which must be believed with divine and catholic faith, or it is likewise an obstinate doubt concerning the same" (CCC 2089).

LUCIFER: The name for the devil that means "light derived from God." Lucifer was created by God as an angel, but rebelled against God's sole authority, and so was driven out of heaven by St. Michael the Archangel and his heavenly army before the creation of man.

MANICHAEISM: A religion popular in Augustine's time that presented the world as a dualistic battleground between a good spiritual world of light and an evil material world of darkness. Founded by the Iranian prophet Mani, it was popular for many centuries and continued until the 14th century in the East. To be free from the shackles of our embodied created nature, Manichaeans promised liberation through secret knowledge (gnosis) of immaterial truths. They advocated abstaining from eating meat and having procreative sex, denying the very goodness of nature and reproduction themselves.

NEOPLATONISM: The philosophical doctrines of Plotinus and his successors, which are based on their own interpretation of Plato's writings. The Neoplatonists professed that happiness could only be found in intellectual, contemplative union with the *logos* or mind of God.

PELAGIANISM: Heresy that denied the existence of original sin and claimed that human beings could achieve moral perfection by an exercise of their own will, without the help of God's grace.

PHILOSOPHY: The study of the fundamental nature of knowledge, reality, and existence, especially when considered as an academic discipline.

ST. AMBROSE: The bishop of Milan and one of the four original Doctors of the Church. Ambrose was the spiritual father of St. Augustine and baptized him in 387 AD. Ambrose captured the attention of St. Augustine right after his arrival in Milan due to his compelling preaching style and content. Ambrose had a deeply philosophical approach, founded especially on Neoplatonism. In addition, his interpretation of Scripture was not totally literal as he used allegorical and symbolic means to explain a lot of Scripture, especially the Old Testament.

STOICISM: An ancient Greek school of philosophy, which taught that virtue, the highest good, is based on knowledge, and that the wise live in harmony with the divine Reason (also identified as Fate and Providence) that governs nature. Stoics strive to be unaffected by either the ups and downs of fortune or the existence of pleasure or pain in life.

VISIGOTHS: The western branches of the barbarian, Germanic tribes referred to collectively as Goths. The Visigoths emerged from the tribes that attacked the Roman Empire beginning in 376. They totally overtook Rome in 410, looting, burning, and destroying everything in their path. For the first time in nearly 1,000 years, the city of Rome was in the hands of non-Romans.

ST. BENEDICT

The Monk

CATHOLICISM
THE PIVOTAL PLAYERS

St. Augustine Study Guide written by Abbot Jeremy Driscoll, O.S.B.

✠

ST. BENEDICT
The Monk

STUDY GUIDE WRITTEN BY
Abbot Jeremy Driscoll, O.S.B.

In 2016, Father Jeremy Driscoll, O.S.B., was elected the 12th abbot of Mount Angel Abbey in Oregon. He has been a Benedictine monk at the same abbey since 1973 and was ordained a priest in 1981. In 1983, he earned an S.T.L. in patristics from the Augustinianum Patristic Institute in Rome. In 1991 he earned an S.T.D. from Sant' Anselmo in Rome.

In 2004, he was named an associate member of the Pontifical Academy of Theology, and in 2010 he was named an "ordinarius" of the same Academy. In 2005 he was appointed by Pope John Paul II as consultor to the Congregation for Divine Worship for a five-year term and Pope Benedict XVI renewed his appointment for another five years. Pope Francis renewed it again in 2017.

Abbot Jeremy is an internationally renowned author and lecturer with books and articles on Egyptian monasticism and Evagrius Ponticus, a Christian monk and ascetic. He has also written widely on liturgical questions and has published three books of poetry.

ST. BENEDICT

The Monk

VIDEO OUTLINE—PART I

I. INTRODUCTION
   A. Most pivotal of all the Pivotal Players
   B. Benedict and his spiritual descendants preserved and grew western culture after fall of Rome
   C. Is there a "Benedict moment" now?

II. LIFE AND TIMES
   A. Early Years
      1. Hagiographic biography of Benedict written by Pope St. Gregory the Great
      2. Born in Nursia, north of Rome, in 480 AD
      3. Sent to Rome for education, but disgusted with moral corruption
      4. Left Rome and went to live in a cave outside Subiaco for three years to commune with God and live an authentic, Christian life
      5. Pattern of retreat, preservation, and reassertion in other ages

   B. Leader of Monastic Communities
      1. Established many small monasteries
      2. Founded Benedictine motherhouse, Monte Cassino, in 530 AD, where he wrote *The Rule*
      3. Died around 545 AD

ST. BENEDICT

LIFE AND TIMES

The only source we have giving information about St. Benedict's biography is in *The Life of St. Benedict* by Pope Gregory the Great, who includes St. Benedict in a larger work about saints called *The Dialogues*. He wrote this around 600 AD as part of his pastoral care of the Church, wanting to impress upon his readers the ideals of sanctity that he felt to be so much needed by all in his flock. The saint to whom he devoted the most space was St. Benedict.

The times were difficult. The Roman Empire and its culture were crumbling around Gregory. This culture was the context in which, in comparatively more stable centuries, the Church had consolidated some of its deepest theological reflections and had achieved an impressive wedding of the Christian message to the best cultural genius of Roman and Greek civilizations. In the West, the future for a Christianity nurtured in this cradle of Roman culture was uncertain given the pressure of barbarian invasions which threatened its achievements. Into this unsettled scene, Pope Gregory recounts the wonderful stories of the life of St. Benedict.

The stories are in a genre called *hagiography*, a technical term for writing about saints, whose style often stresses the fantastic and miraculous. Hagiography is not verifiable history in the way that today we might attempt to write an objective biography of a certain person. Even so, it does express a different kind of truth. It captures the overall impact of a certain saint in image and in feeling. This is what Gregory's image of St. Benedict does. The stories have spiritual messages, and the reader comes to know and enjoy the spirit of the man who acts in them. The spirit of these stories found in *The Life* converges smoothly with the spirit that is found in what is unquestionably the most important source that gives us access to the significance of Benedict as a Pivotal Player—namely, what his followers still call *The Holy Rule*. Referring to *The Rule*, Gregory himself observes that he "could in no way teach other than he lived" (*Life* sec. 16).

That phrase can dictate the plan of this study guide. We will look briefly at how Benedict lived, as recounted in *The Life*. And then we will look more closely at how he taught in *The Rule*. In doing both, we will let his life and teaching challenge us to a deeper living of our own Christian life.

THE LIFE

Gregory summarizes St. Benedict's life on the very first page of *The Life*. Benedict was born in the region of Nursia, north of Rome, around the year 480, shortly after the date generally accepted for the fall of the Empire. He died around the year 540. As a young man, he began studies in Rome but before long was turned off by the immoral atmosphere that surrounded him. He soon retired to live in a nearby wilderness as a hermit.

In the video, Bishop Barron notes that from the fourth through the sixth centuries, many of the best and brightest, in both the East and the West, took, quite literally, to the hills in order to live lives of austerity, poverty, and prayer, far from the corruption of "the world." One thinks of St. John Chrysostom, St. Jerome, St. Gregory of Nyssa, and St. Augustine whose dream, before he was pressed into service as Bishop of Hippo, was to establish a monastery where he and a few others could pursue a life of prayer and study. The spiritual father of all of these figures was St. Anthony of the Desert who, in the third century, had abandoned his comfortable life, given all of his possessions to the poor, and established himself as a hermit in the Egyptian wilderness.

"What was driving these men?" asks Bishop Barron. "It was a deep conviction that the authentic Christian life could not be lived coherently within the ordinary cultural framework of their time. Political confusion, barbarian invasions, and economic instability had a good deal to do with it, but it was also a function of the moral corruption of the period. They felt that they had to create the conditions for a new civilization, precisely by hunkering down, preserving and protecting a form of life which could, in time, influence the wider culture again. The biblical image for this is the Ark of Noah, and we've seen this rhythm often in the history of the Church: retreat, preservation, reassertion."

After three years as a hermit, Benedict was sought out by other monks to lead them as a spiritual father and to organize them into a community-based monastic experience (*Life* sec. 4). Despite ups and downs with the monks who first followed him, he eventually established a very solid form of monastic existence at the monastery called Montecassino. It was here that he wrote *The Rule* (*Life* sec. 16).

The stories that recount these developments are easily read. It is best to allow them to exert their charm, not wondering too much or worrying if such amazing stories could be literally true as told. Benedict very likely did bless others with miraculous deeds. So the reader should simply let the impact of the story deliver the impact of the man Benedict. A brief analysis of two stories can show us how to do this. This will also allow us to see that the stories are relevant even now, 1500 years later, to our situation and growth as Christians.

"The Rough Goth Named Zalla" (*Life* sec. 13) is a story about the barbarian world meeting St. Benedict. St. Benedict is engaged in an activity that characterizes the form of monasticism he created. He is doing *lectio divina*, that is, he was engaged in slow and prayerful meditation on Scripture. Zalla, the Goth, is vividly described as a man who "burned with an insane hatred... inflamed with the heat of avarice and panting for rapine." He is afflicting a poor peasant, who has the good sense to tell Zalla that the goods with which he can repay this greedy man are deposited with St. Benedict at the monastery. In the story we're not told if this is true or not, but the peasant's thought surely was that if he could get this barbarian anywhere near St. Benedict, the saint could probably help him. Indeed, he does.

The poor peasant is bound with thongs and led to the monastery. When they arrive, Benedict is described as "sitting alone and reading at the entrance of the house." Unmoved by this peaceful atmosphere and pose of the saint, the barbarian shouts at him and tells him to "fork over the goods of this lousy peasant." Benedict's reaction is altogether calm. He simply looks up from his reading and casts his gaze on Zalla and then soon after on the poor peasant. It's important to catch the scene created by the careful telling of the narrator. This is a monk looking up from Scripture and seeing before him the broken world of sinful, cruel, mean-spirited behavior in other human beings. The monk's glance is filled with the vision and power of Scripture. It is extremely powerful and is just what is needed. We read: "His glance fell on his bound arms, and the shackles began to loosen faster than any human hand could have undone them." Zalla is terrified by this power and casts himself at Benedict's feet. Benedict does not take much note of this, for he is determined to remain anchored in his reading of Scripture. But he does tell some of the other monks to take him inside and provide him with a little refreshment. When he comes back out again, Benedict simply tells him not to treat others so cruelly.

The lesson is still relevant to us today. In a world filled with rough talk and manners, with "insane hatred" and "the heat of avarice," the Christian is invited to gaze at this world with a glance shaped by Scripture and the Good News it recounts. That glance can make a huge difference. It can set others free and keep us rooted in peace.

"The Whole World in a Single Ray of Sunlight" (*Life* sec. 15) is another wonderful story that took place toward the end of Benedict's life. It is the final story that Gregory tells before recounting the story of Benedict's death. This story has instructed generations of monks about the relationship between prayer and the world, and it can offer us the same valuable lesson today.

"Standing at the window and praying to almighty God in the middle of the night, he [Benedict] suddenly saw a light pour down that routed all the shadows. It shone with such splendor that it surpassed daylight, even though it was shining in the darkness....The whole world was brought before his eyes as if collected in a single ray of sunlight." This storytelling style wants us to imagine the scene, but it is hard to do so. We are to wonder at the paradox: something brighter than sunlight but shining in darkness and the whole world "collected" to be seen in a single glance. How is this possible? Gregory offers a sublime explanation. He says, "The soul becomes greater than itself through contemplation. For when the contemplative soul is ravished by the light of God, it is dilated." What a vision of prayer is offered here! The soul at prayer grows larger than the whole world and can contain it within its loving glance.

For centuries this image has shaped the imagination of monks, calling them to a prayer that seeks to embrace the whole world in the light of Christ. Such a vision, Gregory explains, does not mean that heaven and earth are shrunk but that the soul is expanded. Christian prayer is —astounding claim!—bigger than the whole world and can contain it all in a loving glance.

When we hear of a vision like St. Benedict's, we should not at once react by dismissing it as beyond ourselves. In the last lines of *The Rule*, Benedict calls it a "little rule that we have written for beginners" (*The Rule*, chap. 73). That could be any one of us. A way of life can lead to prayer larger than the world.

THE FATHER OF ALL MONKS:
ST. ANTHONY *of the* DESERT

Known as the founder of Christian monasticism, St. Anthony was the first to live a solitary life of prayer and asceticism away from any community. Before St. Anthony, Christians had devoted themselves to prayer, fasting, celibacy, and self-denial, but none had ever left family and home to do so.

Most of what we know of St. Anthony is from the *Life of Anthony*, written in the fourth century by St. Athanasius of Alexandria. Anthony was born in 251 AD in Coma, Egypt. When he was only 8 years old, his parents died and left him a vast inheritance. When he was 20, he heard the story of the rich, young man in Matthew's Gospel, and felt Jesus was talking to him when he said, "If you wish to be perfect, go, sell what you have and give to the poor, and you will have treasure in heaven. Then come, follow me" (Matt 19:21). He promptly sold everything and left his privileged life to live in a tomb on the outskirts of town. He lived there for fifteen years, visiting other hermits who lived on the perimeter to learn about their way of life and the graces they received.

Then, craving even more solitude, Anthony traveled far from Coma to make his home in an old, abandoned fort in the desert. He lived there completely alone for twenty years, subsisting on donations of food that pilgrims threw over the wall of the fort when they came to seek him out.

As in the case of St. Benedict, Anthony struggled to retain his solitude. When Anthony refused to see or talk to pilgrims, many eventually took up residence in huts and caves around the old fort. They pleaded with him to come out to teach and guide them as their leader. Finally, Anthony agreed to leave his life of solitude to shepherd those who had encamped around him, causing him to be known as the "Father of All Monks."

For about five or six years, he lived with these disciples, instructing and guiding them. But then the need for solitude overcame him and he left his flock to travel and take up residence on a mountain in the Sahara Desert between the Nile and the Red Sea. On this mountain, a Coptic Orthodox monastery still stands that bears his name: *Der Mar Antonios*. He spent the last forty-five years of his life alone on that mountain but was willing to talk with those who came to see him. He also traveled a bit—twice to Alexandria. The first trip in 311 was to support the persecuted Christians who were being martyred there, and the second in 350 was to preach against the Arian heresy. Anthony died shortly thereafter at the age of 105.

His writings speak of the duties of the spiritual life, especially the battle with evil, which he personally experienced. When he was first living in the tomb near his village, evil spirits often took the form of wild beasts to inflict pain upon him, make him unconscious, and bring him near death.

Blessed John Henry Newman wrote of Anthony's character in his book, *Church of the Fathers*: "His doctrine surely was pure and unimpeachable; and his temper is high and heavenly, without cowardice, without gloom, without formality, without self-complacency. Superstition is abject and crouching, it is full of thoughts of guilt; it distrusts God, and dreads the powers of evil. Anthony at least had nothing of this, being full of confidence, divine peace, cheerfulness, and valorousness, be he (as some men may judge) ever so much an enthusiast."

LECTIO DIVINA

Lectio divina is a form of meditative prayer based on Scripture that St. Benedict used and recommended frequently. Here is an overview of how you can pray using *Lectio divina*.

1. Set aside a short period (10-15 minutes) for *lectio divina*. Relax and get comfortable in a quiet place. Begin by resting in silence for a minute or two.

2. Select a passage from Scripture on which to reflect. Many people choose the upcoming Gospel reading for Sunday Mass, which you can find online or in the daily Missal.

3. Read your chosen passage slowly and carefully. Pay special attention to any word or phrase that speaks to you, one that interests you more than the rest. The goal is not merely to consume information but to recognize God's prompting. As we center our mind on the text, and carefully listen for God's stirring, we can move deeply into his presence through his word.

4. Repeat the word or phrase you identified in the previous step to yourself. You may even want to repeat the word quietly out loud, allowing it to sink into your mind and heart. During this step, pay special attention to any thoughts or feelings that arise as you reflect on the chosen word or phrase.

5. In a spirit of prayer, talk to the Lord about these thoughts and feelings just as you would a good friend. Share with God your reaction to his Word, and ask him to lead you to even deeper reflection.

6. Finally, in response to your request, expect God to respond in his "still, small voice." Listen for him. Be attuned to any words, images, or feelings that arise during this time of restful listening.

7. Sometimes your *lectio divina* period may be consumed with reflection on a single word or phrase. Other times, you may need to return to the passage and keep reading to see if something else stands out. There's no right or wrong way. And there's no goal, other than to experience God's presence and reflect on his word.

HOW MONKS PRESERVED WESTERN CIVILIZATION

Historical scholars have amended the negative title of "Dark Ages" to include only 500 to 700 AD, which were the centuries that turned back the advance of Western civilization. That's when Roman civilization, as we know it, collapsed. Without the Church, we would have no record or remnant of the amazingly advanced Roman culture.

The establishment of Western monasticism by St. Benedict saved and advanced European culture. Benedict did not set out with this goal in mind, but it happened through the efforts of his and other monks.

In addition to spiritual activities, monks engaged in and developed agriculture and the practical arts. Manual labor was an intrinsic part of their rule, which proclaimed "ora et labora" (pray and work). They literally saved agriculture in Europe. Monks taught land cultivation, and introduced crops, industries, and production methods with which the people were not yet familiar (e.g., breeding cattle, brewing beer). Monks established corn trading in Sweden, cheese making in Parma, salmon fisheries in Ireland, and vineyards everywhere. Water power was harnessed for crushing wheat, sifting flour, and making cloth. Monasteries were the most economically effective units that had ever existed in Europe. Not even the Romans had industrialized to such an extent.

But the one occupation that perhaps more than any other helped in the preservation of Western civilization was the copying of ancient manuscripts. It began in the sixth century at a monastery in southern Italy, which housed a fine library where the copying of manuscripts took center stage. Thereafter, most monasteries were endowed with so-called *scriptoria* as part of their libraries: rooms where ancient literature was transcribed by monks as part of their daily labor.

The monks' devotion to books was so extraordinary that they would travel far and wide in search of rare manuscripts. A monk of Muri said it all: "Without study and without books, the life of a monk is nothing." So, we can confidently say that Western civilization's admiration for the written word and the classics of antiquity *have come to us via the Catholic Church*, which preserved them throughout the barbarian invasions.

Schools associated with the medieval cathedrals also preserved manuscripts and fostered education. These schools laid the groundwork for the first university established at Bologna in the eleventh century. Many nobles were sent to monastery schools to be educated, including Thomas Aquinas, who was educated at Montecassino. St. Benedict himself instructed the sons of Roman nobles; St. Boniface established a school in every German monastery he founded; and the same was done by St. Augustine and by St. Patrick.

The monks' commitment to reading, writing, and education ensured the survival of Western civilization after unceasing barbarian invasions. Monks laid the foundations for European universities and became the bridge between antiquity and modernity. Thus, it is a great fallacy to assert that the Church encouraged the destruction of ancient pagan culture. On the contrary, she helped preserve that culture, which would have otherwise been lost.

— Adapted from "Medieval Monasticism as Preserver of Western Civilization" by Emmanuel Paparella published on metanexus.net (May 31, 2008).

QUESTIONS FOR UNDERSTANDING

1. Bishop Barron says that St. Benedict may be the most pivotal of all the Pivotal Players. Why?

   - brought back Christian ways

2. What drove St. Benedict away from Rome as a young man? Where did he go and why did he choose that place?

3. What similarities do you see between St. Anthony of the Desert and St. Benedict? What conclusions can you draw about the attributes of a holy person based on these similarities? (CCC 2013-2015)

4. The three years that St. Benedict spent in the cave of Subiaco were a time of "gestation and spiritual deepening," according to Bishop Barron. What examples can you find in Scripture of people who also spent time alone before embarking on a particular mission? Why is it so important to spend time in solitude before taking on God's work? (Matt 4:1-22; Gal 1:11-24; Rev 1:9-20; CCC 538, 921)

5. What is *lectio divina*? How can you better understand St. Benedict's actions when you know that he practiced *lectio divina* regularly? (CCC 2653-2654)

6. Those who live the monastic life spend much time in contemplative prayer. What are the key steps and components of contemplative prayer? (CCC 2709-2719)

QUESTIONS FOR APPLICATION

1. How can you, as a lay person, put some of the practices of monks into your daily life? Why is it important to do so?

2. When writing about St. Benedict, St. Gregory the Great said, "The soul becomes greater than itself through contemplation. For when the contemplative soul is ravished by the light of God, it is dilated." What does this mean in your own words? Have you ever experienced this sort of enlargement of your own soul? If so, describe it.

3. Look up the Gospel for next Sunday and practice *lectio divina* using that Gospel. (See Sidebar on page 46 for an explanation of *lectio divina*.)

NOTES:

ST. BENEDICT

The Monk

VIDEO OUTLINE—PART II

I. PURPOSE OF *THE RULE*
   A. Governed monasteries and monks' way of life
   B. Relevant to those who seek to create a more humane and well-ordered society
   C. Other "rules" influenced Benedict: St. Anthony of the Desert, Augustine, St. Basil and Cassian
   D. Not just spiritually uplifting—it works

II. OVERVIEW OF *THE RULE*
   A. Starts simply with one word, *Obsculta*—listen
      1. Human history of not listening to the Word on God
      2. Salvation history begins with Abraham, who listened to the Lord
      3. Addressed to those who are willing to renounce own will and obey God
      4. Listen to a higher voice, let in the light
      5. Can create a "school of the Lord's service"
   B. Types of Monks
      1. Cenobites: live in community
      2. Anchorites: those who are trained in monastic community and then become hermits
      3. Sarabaites: live in small groups without abbot or rule
      4. Gyrovagues: monks who wander from community to community, following their own will and pleasures
   C. The Abbot
      1. Derived from Hebrew term, *Abba*, the affectionate term for father
      2. Abbot is father and monks are brothers to one another
      3. Concerned only with the advancement of all in good works
      4. When making a major decision, he is to consult with *all* the brothers
      5. Monks acquire spiritual tutelage from abbot
   D. Humility
      1. Fear of God, knowing God sees all

2. Love God's will, not your own

3. Always submit to one's superior in obedience

4. Obey in silence even when burden is hard or unjust

5. Confess all, even internal thoughts, to abbot

6. Be satisfied with one's conditions and circumstances

7. Monk proclaims and believes in his heart that he is lowest of all brothers

8. Do not do anything unless it is proscribed by *The Rule* or ordered by abbot; no self-assertion

9. Keep silent until someone asks you something

10. Do not be inclined or prompt to laugh

11. Express yourself calmly, reasonably, and without raising your voice

12. Keep head down and eyes fixed on the ground, feeling weight of sin

E. Prayer

   1. Monks pray formally seven times each day

      a. Drop whatever they are doing and hasten to prayer

      b. Based on the psalms

   2. Prefer nothing to the "work of God," which is prayer

F. Work

   1. Ordinary work offers praise to the Lord

   2. "Laziness is the enemy of the soul"

   3. Defined as manual labor and spiritual reading

   4. All the monks work, no matter rank or age

G. Other Features of *The Rule*

   1. Priority of the community; life in common

   2. Radical poverty; no private property

   3. Hospitality

      a. "All guests should be received as Christ"—see Christ in each guest

      b. Hasten to greet a guest and show every mark of respect

      c. Accompany visitors at prayer

      d. Break the fast to eat hospitably with guest

III. CONCLUSION

A. Radical life of *The Rule* meant to echo life as described in Acts of the Apostles and anticipate fullness of community in heaven

B. Benedict and his brothers preserved what was best in classical culture and used it for future development and propagation of Christianity

ST. BENEDICT

THE RULE

The Rule is not a long document, but it is thick with wisdom and generally is best absorbed in small doses. In most monasteries, a small portion of the *The Rule* is read aloud every day to the whole community. Slowly but surely its wisdom sinks in. This can be a good way for any of us to come to understand it. That can perhaps justify the method we adopt in this study guide. We will take a sampling of passages treating different attitudes and concrete practices that St. Benedict asked his monks to cultivate.

A SCHOOL FOR THE LORD'S SERVICE
Prologue of The Rule

At the end of the stirring Prologue of *The Rule,* Benedict writes, "Therefore we intend to establish a school for the Lord's service. In drawing up its regulations, we hope to set down nothing harsh, nothing burdensome" (*The Rule* Prol. 45). The image of school has had a strong impact on the monastic imagination. A person goes to school to learn something, and a certain amount of discipline is necessary. Benedict admits this, but he does not want discipline for discipline's sake. A monastery is not army boot camp where soldiers are toughened up by intentionally harsh treatment. Even so, Benedict says that in this school there will be need for "a little strictness" (*The Rule* Prol. 47). But we should note carefully the reason. It is "to amend faults and to safeguard love" (*The Rule* Prol. 47). Those are the areas in which Benedict's school can help us make progress. And he adds an attractive goal for the "little strictness" that this school requires. He says, "As we progress in this way of life and in faith, we shall run on the path of God's commandments, our hearts overflowing with the inexpressible delight of love" (*The Rule* Prol. 49). It is a life in which one makes progress, and doing so, the heart expands and tastes the sweetness of love. As the rest of *The Rule* unfolds, the reader will come to see that "a school for the Lord's service" does not simply mean serving the Lord but learning to serve as the Lord himself served us. For Benedict shapes his pupils into imitators of Christ precisely in Christ's humility and his willingness to serve. Christ came "to serve, not to be served" (Matt 20:28). Learning this is Benedict's "school for the Lord's service."

HOW TO ATTEND A MEETING
Chapter 3 of The Rule

Chapter 3 of the *Rule* is titled "Summoning the Brothers for Counsel." Short as it is, it is full of wise advice for the abbot about how to consult the monks for their insights on important matters as well as advice on how the monks should offer their own points of view. The mood that this chapter establishes could serve us well in our own times as advice on how to participate in a meeting. What Benedict stipulates helps a community to avoid contention, even while living with different opinions. "As often as anything important is to be done in the monastery, the abbot shall call the whole community together and himself explain what the business is; and after hearing the advice of the brothers, let him ponder it and follow what he judges the wiser course" (*The Rule* 3:1-2). What is clear here is that one person is in charge—the abbot—but the advice of all is genuinely to be taken into consideration. A measure of how serious Benedict is about this is the reason he gives for the abbot listening to everyone: because "the Lord often reveals what is better to the younger" (*The Rule* 3:3). This would have been revolutionary in the Roman culture of the fifth and sixth centuries, where generally only elders were considered to carry wisdom. Not so in *The Rule*, where—just as in the Christian message itself—we are taught to be ready to expect blessings from the least and the smallest.

Benedict goes on to say something important about how the monks are to contribute their insights: "The brothers...are to express their opinions with all humility, and not presume to defend their own views obstinately" (*The Rule* 3:4). This perhaps contrasts sharply with our own culture's style of speaking one's point of view. We are tempted to push and force it. Benedict instead wants an atmosphere of discernment to pervade a community meeting, so that no matter what is decided there will be peace in the group. "The decision is rather the abbot's to make, so that when he has determined what is more prudent, all may obey" (*The Rule* 3:5).

Benedict knows that this obedience may not always be easy or come naturally. So he warns, "In the monastery no one is to follow his own heart's desire, nor shall anyone presume to contend with his abbot defiantly, or outside the monastery" (*The Rule* 3:8-9). What we see here is Benedict's school in action. He says "in the monastery," as if to emphasize that we are going to live differently here, that we will not follow our natural tendencies to win in every situation, no matter what it takes. Placing the final decision in the abbot's hands certainly puts a burden on him, but it is an arrangement that should result in peace for the whole community. The abbot himself is reassured in his burden by Benedict's final word, which is a citation from Scripture: "*Do everything with counsel and you will not be sorry afterward* (Sir 32:19)" (*The Rule* 3:13).

ON RESTRAINT IN SPEECH OR THE IMPORTANCE OF SILENCE
Chapter 6 of The Rule

People expect a monastery to be a silent place and rightly so. Benedict stresses silence throughout *The Rule*. But why silence? What is it for? Benedict explains, "Indeed, so important is silence that permission to speak should seldom be granted even to mature disciples, no matter how good or holy or constructive their talk, because it is written: *In a flood of words you will not avoid sin* (Prov 10:19)" (*The Rule* 6:3-4). This kind of advice challenges us, especially to think that Benedict is reluctant even to allow positive talk. What he is trying to cultivate in the monk—and in anyone who would follow his teaching—is a receptive attitude, a letting-go of the possibilities of control in a situation, something to which even our good talk can be unwittingly directed. Silence, instead, disposes us to hear God, whose word and presence comes to us from different sources. It comes from the Scripture and our silent meditation on it. It comes from the silence itself, which can attune us to God's constant presence and his presence everywhere. It comes from the abbot's word or another's word.

Benedict says, "Speaking and teaching are the master's task; the disciple is to be silent and listen" (*The Rule* 6:6). Benedict is inviting us to be disciples, which he defines as being silent and listening. With silence as the atmosphere of the whole monastery, the disciple can grow in humility and will more and more be caught up in the prayer, which is simple awareness of God's presence and God addressing a "word" to me. I am ready to receive it gratefully and in humility.

HUMILITY—NOT HIDING FROM GOD'S LIGHT OF TRUTH
Chapter 7 of The Rule

Unquestionably, one of the most important parts of *The Rule* is the long chapter on humility. This is a core monastic virtue that the school of Benedict's monastery wants to teach. Without doing the work that is asked by Benedict in this chapter, the life of a monk loses its interior dimension, its soul. The language of this chapter is something we are not used to, and we instinctively shy away from it. But we would do well to let ourselves be challenged by it.

Benedict delineates twelve steps of humility, calling them a ladder; and he plays with the paradox of claiming that we climb the ladder by descending. Here he is half-quoting the Lord who said, "Whoever exalts himself shall be humbled, and whoever humbles himself shall be exalted" (Luke 14:11 in *The Rule* 7:1). The reader of this study guide is invited to read and ponder all twelve steps as summarized in the sidebar on pages 66-67.

A few keys can help us to absorb the challenge that Benedict launches. One key can be found in the first step, which is about living our lives completely aware that all that we do and think and say is done in the presence of God. Nearly all of us tend to forget this and even cultivate habits that help us to forget. But this is not living in reality. Benedict says, "let [the monk] recall that he is always seen by God in heaven, that his actions everywhere are in God's sight and are reported by angels at every hour" (*The Rule* 7:13). We can be annoyed by talk like this, presenting God and angels as if they were spying on us. But if we consider this a bit, we would have to admit that such annoyance is not entirely innocent. If annoyance is our response, that is still the residue of original sin in us. After the fall, Adam and Eve attempted to hide from God. Benedict is reminding his monks that such hiding is not possible and doesn't conform to reality. Benedict's own experience lies behind this formulation. In the *Life* by Gregory we read, "Then he returned to his beloved place of solitude, where he lived alone with himself but under the gaze of the Heavenly Spectator" (*Life* sec. 3). Gregory then spins out a long development of what living with oneself in the sight of God would mean.

Another key to understanding all of the steps of humility is to realize that by them Benedict is giving his monks a program that will conform them to the humility that Jesus Christ himself displayed his whole life, "who though he was in the form of God...humbled himself, becoming obedient to death, even death on a cross" (Phil 2:6,8). This biblical text stands behind the second, third, and fourth steps of humility, but also the sixth and the seventh. Again, we shy away from some of the language we encounter in these steps. For example, Benedict wants the monk to put in his mouth the words of the psalmist who says, "I am insignificant and ignorant " (Ps 73:22 in *The Rule* 7:50) or "I am truly a worm, not a man" (Ps 22:7 in *The Rule* 7:52). We will take the lesson a little more seriously if we realize that such verses describe our Lord himself in his passion, and that Benedict is teaching us to imitate him. With these steps we are made to encounter our sinful reality, and what we would be if not for God's constant mercy in our lives.

Learning such lessons in humility will eventually result not only in the interior but in the exterior transformation of a monk, affecting the very ways in which he speaks and walks (Steps 9, 10, 11, and 12). Humility builds a whole culture and style of life. It is meant to emanate from a monk in the whole of life, so that "a monk always manifests humility in his bearing no less than in his heart, so that it is evident at the Work of God, in the oratory, the monastery or the garden, on a journey or in the field, or anywhere else " (*The Rule* 7:62-63). In this list, prayer ("the Work of God," which is Benedict's name for the community prayer) is the radiant center of a monk's humility, but it reaches outward from there to every other part of the monastery and to well beyond it, to "anywhere."

TREATING TOOLS LIKE
SACRED VESSELS OF THE ALTAR
Chapter 31 of The Rule

Chapter 31 of the *The Rule* on the "Qualifications of the Monastery Cellarer" might surprise someone who is expecting a monastic rule to treat only lofty spiritual questions. "Cellarer" is the old monastic term for the monk charged with helping the abbot to care for all the material concerns of a monastery. What is striking in this very carefully crafted chapter is that we see that all the *material* concerns that keep a monastery up and running are in fact also *spiritual* questions. So, whomever the abbot appoints to this work must be "wise, mature in conduct, temperate, not an excessive eater, not proud, excitable, offensive, dilatory or wasteful" (*The Rule* 31:1). It is evident that these are characteristics that would be to the advantage of anyone entrusted with the practical, material, day-to-day concerns of a group of human beings trying to live together in community for a lifetime. Here again a whole culture is being created by the way the monks will live and relate to one another. Benedict foresees that a monk might "make an unreasonable demand" of the cellarer. He suggests that the response should be a gentle introducing of reality into the scene. He says that the cellarer "should not reject him with disdain and cause him distress, but reasonably and humbly deny the improper request" (*The Rule* 31:7).

Perhaps the sentence from this chapter that most clearly puts into relief the understanding that *material* questions have a *spiritual* dimension is how Benedict asks the cellarer to care for the tools and equipment of the monastery. He says, "He will regard all utensils and goods of the monastery as sacred vessels of the altar" (*The Rule* 31:10). So, it is not just when the monks are in church praying that the spiritual project is underway. Every part of the day and each thing in the day is sacred because God is present everywhere, and the monk is to be constantly cultivating mindfulness of this fact.

THE RHYTHM BETWEEN
MANUAL LABOR & READING
Chapter 48 of The Rule

There are many prescriptions in the *Rule* about how practical things are to be arranged. Through the centuries monks have not necessarily followed these in literal detail, but such chapters contain principles that monks still use for how best to pass the hours of any given day. One such chapter is titled "The Daily Manual Labor." It begins with a dictum: "Idleness is the enemy of the soul." Then it continues: "Therefore, the brothers should have specified periods for manual labor as well as for prayerful reading [*lectio divina*]" (*The Rule* 48:1). Although the title mentions only manual labor, in fact this chapter deals with the use of time in general. Monks are meant to work hard. For example, Benedict says, "When they live by the labor of their hands, as our fathers and the apostles did, then they are really monks" (*The Rule* 48:8). A second, but just as important, monastic practice outlined here is the well-known practice of *lectio divina*. At least several hours of every day are to be devoted to *lectio divina*. Such prayerful reading plus manual labor make for a balanced and disciplined day. Such rhythms, practiced day by day, month after month, year by year is what formed monasteries and monks into great shapers of culture and societies throughout the centuries. Similar rhythms suggest themselves still today as good practices for families and for other types of communities, not to mention for individual Christians who want their lives marked by monasticism's practical wisdom.

ON HOSPITALITY
Chapter 53 of The Rule

One of the most influential and characteristic chapters of the *Rule* is titled "The Reception of Guests." Benedict begins the long chapter forcefully. He says, "All guests who present themselves are to be welcomed as Christ" (*The Rule* 53:1) By this he means not simply that the monks should treat guests as they might treat Christ if he himself were to visit. Benedict's point is stronger. He means that the monks are to perceive the presence of Christ himself coming in the guests. He justifies this sense by quoting Christ's own words, addressing them to his monks: "For he [Christ] himself will say: *I was a stranger and you welcomed me* (Matt 25:35)" (*The Rule* 53:1). So far from monks being instructed to beware of guests or to count them a disturbance, Benedict sees guests at the monastery as a special grace. He speaks about how to receive them and how to say goodbye, enjoining, "All humility should be shown in addressing a guest on arrival or departure. By a bow of the head or by a complete prostration of the body, Christ is to be adored because he is indeed welcomed in them" (*The Rule* 53:6-7). Next, guests are invited to pray with the monks, the Scriptures are read for their instruction, and then "every kindness [*Omnis humanitas*]" is shown to them (*The Rule* 53:8-9) —literally from the Latin, "all humanity." In monastic vocabulary *umanitas* became a monastic expression for a good meal given to guests. The monks themselves on many days observed different rules about food, sometimes keeping a fast until a certain hour. But Benedict says, "The superior may break his fast for the sake of a guest" (*Rule* 53:10).

There is something wonderful in all this. Through the centuries such careful, overly generous, and gracious hospitality extended by monks to strangers at no cost and with no expectations surprised guests and imparted to them, often unexpectedly, the monastic gift of peace. Such hospitality is an implicit preaching of the Gospel and often the first deep evangelizing "word" that a person might ever hear. People still need to be met by good Christians with this same kind of generous hospitality.

ACT IN ALL GENTLENESS
Chapter 66 of The Rule

Another chapter, "The Porter of the Monastery," adds something to all this that could be extended as advice to any Christian on how to respond to an unexpected summons or request. Benedict envisions a monk being placed at the door of the monastery: "As soon as anyone knocks, or a poor man calls out, he replies, 'Thanks be to God' or 'Your blessing, please'; then, with all the gentleness that comes from the fear of God, he provides a prompt answer with the warmth of love" (*The Rule* 66:3-4). We could all measure ourselves perhaps against this monastic ideal of the porter. To bring it to our times: when the phone rings, or there is a knock on the door, or we receive a request of some sort—what if we were immediately to respond "Thanks be to God" to that and to give a prompt answer with the warmth of love? This could very much change the kind of world in which we live. By it Benedict changed his world. This was the same attitude with which he met the angry Goth at the monastery door and so managed to set the poor peasant free.

THE GOOD ZEAL OF MONKS
Chapter 72 of the Rule

The penultimate chapter of *The Rule* is a lovely finale to the kind of teaching we have sampled here and of which the entire document is full. Perhaps it is enough simply to invite the user of this study guide to read this chapter's beautiful lines as a summary of all we have touched upon here. It needs little comment:

> Just as there is a wicked zeal of bitterness which separates from God and leads to hell, so there is a good zeal which separates from evil and leads to God and everlasting life. This, then, is the good zeal which monks must foster with fervent love: *They should each try to be the first to show respect to the other* (Rom 12:10), Supporting with the greatest patience one another's weaknesses of body or behavior, and earnestly competing in obedience to one another. No one is to pursue what he judges better for himself, but instead, what he judges better for someone else. To their fellow monks they show the pure love of brothers; to God, loving fear; to their abbot, unfeigned and humble love. Let them prefer nothing whatever to Christ, and may he bring us all together to everlasting life (*The Rule* 72:1-12).

THE 12 STEPS *of* HUMILITY

St. Benedict describes the ladder of humility as the direct opposite of the ladder of worldly success, in that we will "descend by exaltation and ascend by humility."

The twelve steps from Chapter 7 of *The Rule* are summarized as follows:

1. Keep the fear of God ever before your eyes and recall that you are always seen by God and that your actions everywhere are in God's sight. (Ps 36:1-3)

2. Love not your own will and do not take pleasure in the satisfaction of your desires, but seek to do the will of God always. (John 6:38)

3. Be obedient to those in authority over you for the love of God. (Phil 2:8)

4. In this obedience, if suffering occurs from difficult, unfavorable, or even unjust conditions, embrace the suffering silently and patiently and do not seek to escape. (Matt 10:22)

5. Do not conceal any sinful thoughts or wrongs but confess them humbly. (Ps 37:5)

6. Be content with the lowest and most menial treatment and living conditions, regarding yourself as a poor and worthless workman in whatever task is given. (Ps 73:22-23)

7. Admit with your tongue and be convinced in your heart that you are inferior to all and of less value than anyone. (Ps 22:6)

8. Do what is lawful and follow the example set by your elders.

9. Control your tongue and remain silent, not speaking unless asked a question. (Prov 10:19)

10. Do not be given to ready laughter. (Sir 21:20)

11. Speak gently and seriously with few words and without raising your voice.

12. Manifest humility in your bearing as well as in your heart with bowed head and eyes cast down, feeling the weight of your sins. (Luke 18:13)

1. Describe Benedict's "school of the Lord's service" and its goal (Matt 20:26-28).

2. What is the opening word of *The Rule* and why is it so important? What role does silence have in living out this instruction? (Deut 6:4; 1 Kings 19:11-13; Matt 7:24; Rom 10:17; James 1:19)

3. What is the role of discipline in the "school of the Lord's service"?
    (Prov 10:17; Heb 12:7-11; Rev 3:19)

4. What is *The Rule's* most highly prized virtue? Why? (Phil 2:3, 5-11;
    Prov 11:2, 22:4; 1 Pet 5:5-6)

5. Why is hospitality so important to Benedict? Describe some aspects of this hospitality. (Matt 25:35, 1 John 4:20, Heb 13:1-2)

6. What are the three things that Benedictine monks, no matter what their rank, are expected to do each day? What is the purpose of those activities? (1 Thess 5:17; CCC 133, 2427-2428, 2687)

QUESTIONS FOR APPLICATION

1. Review the sidebar on pages 66-67, *The 12 Steps of Humility*. Which one or two steps stand out as the most challenging? Why? What can you do to incorporate the spirit of those steps into your daily life?

2. Our culture values individuality over obedience. Which do you value more? To whom and how are you called to be obedient?

3. Next time you are disturbed by an unexpected interruption, notice how you respond. Then think about *The Rule's* direction to say, "Thanks be to God," and then to give a prompt answer with the warmth of love.

4. How can *The Rule* create a more humane and well-ordered life for you and for society in general?

GLOSSARY

ABBOT: the leader and spiritual father of a monastery. Derived from the Hebrew word, *Abba*, an affectionate term for "father"

ANCHORITES: St. Benedict's term for monks trained in monastic community and then set out as hermits to face "the solitary combat of the desert" (*The Rule* 1:3)

CELLARER: a monk in a monastery who is responsible for all objects and possessions of the monastery

CENOBITES: St. Benedict's term for monks living in community (*The Rule* 1:2); the monks that he clearly favors

CONTEMPLATIVE PRAYER: an inner, silent, and intense "gaze of faith, fixed on Jesus" (CCC 2715) whereby, through grace, we are conformed to the likeness of God. St. Teresa of Avila said that contemplative prayer was a "close sharing between friends" and "taking time frequently to be alone with him who we know loves us" (CCC 2709)

DIALOGUES OF ST. GREGORY THE GREAT: a book written by Pope Gregory about fifty years after the death of St. Benedict that is the source of the limited biographical information about Benedict

GYROVAGUES: St. Benedict's term for monks who wander from community to community, and "they never settle down, and are slaves to their own wills and gross appetites" (*The Rule* 1:11)

HAGIOGRAPHY: a technical term for writing about saints, whose style often stresses the fantastic and miraculous

LECTIO DIVINA: praying with and through Scripture (see Sidebar on page 46)

MONTE CASSINO: the Benedictine monastery founded by St. Benedict southeast of Rome that exists today as the motherhouse of the worldwide Benedictine family

OBSCULTA: the opening word of *The Rule*, which means "listen"

ORA ET LABORA: the Benedictine motto, which means "pray and work"

SARABAITES: St. Benedict's term for monks who live in small groups without an abbot or a guiding rule of life (*The Rule* 1:6-9)